THE SCIENCE OF FUN

T0025114

THE SCIENCE OF
AMUSEMENT PARKS

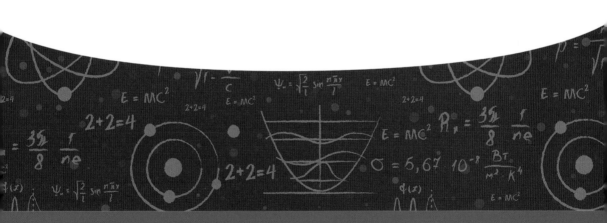

BY DOUGLAS HUSTAD

CONTENT CONSULTANT
David Lamp, PhD
Associate Professor, Department of Physics and Astronomy
Texas Tech University

Cover image: Roller coaster designers use science to make thrilling
yet safe rides.

Core Library

An Imprint of Abdo Publishing
abdobooks.com

abdobooks.com

Printed in the United States of America, North Mankato, Minnesota
052021
092021

 THIS BOOK CONTAINS
RECYCLED MATERIALS

Cover Photo: Shutterstock Images
Interior Photos: Debbie Egan-Chin/NY Daily News Archive/Getty Images, 4–5; Tim Larsen/
AP Images, 7; Panagiotis Kotsovolos/Alamy, 8; Shutterstock Images, 11 (left), 11 (right), 14–15,
24–25, 31, 32, 45; Bika Ambon/iStockphoto, 11 (center); iStockphoto, 12; Tommy Alven/Shutterstock
Images, 17, 43; Red Line Editorial, 21; Justus Sustermans/Newscom, 27; Richard Ellis/Zuma Press/
Newscom, 28; Uladzimir Gudvin/Shutterstock Images, 34–35; Patrick T. Fallon/Bloomberg/Getty
Images, 37; Jeff Gritchen/Orange County Register/MediaNews Group/Getty Images, 39

Editor: Marie Pearson
Series Designer: Katharine Hale

Library of Congress Control Number: 2020948345

Publisher's Cataloging-in-Publication Data

Names: Hustad, Douglas, author.
Title: The science of amusement parks / by Douglas Hustad
Description: Minneapolis, Minnesota : Abdo Publishing, 2022 | Series: The science of fun | Includes
    online resources and index.
Identifiers: ISBN 9781532195150 (lib. bdg.) | ISBN 9781644946091 (pbk.) |
    ISBN 9781098215460 (ebook)
Subjects: LCSH: Amusement parks--Juvenile literature. | Force and energy--Juvenile literature. |
    Physics--Juvenile literature. | Dynamics--Juvenile literature. | Motion--Juvenile literature.
Classification: DDC 531.1--dc23

CONTENTS

RIDING KINGDA KA

The line moves slowly for the Kingda Ka roller coaster. It is the top attraction at the Six Flags Great Adventure and Safari amusement park in New Jersey. Kingda Ka is the world's tallest roller coaster. It is also one of the fastest. Sometimes its riders wait in line for more than an hour in the summer heat. There are few attractions that would make people wait this long.

The line may be slow, but the ride is anything but. Riders take their seats in one of

Kingda Ka's speed thrills riders.

the cars of the roller coaster's train and strap in. As the train moves into position, riders see what they're in for. The ride's 456-foot (140-m) peak lies ahead. Green steel seems to soar forever into the sky. Kingda Ka is named for a Bengal tiger. The ride itself is like a jungle cat waiting to pounce.

An automated voice warns riders to hang on. The train's brakes release with a hiss. Riders wait with no idea when their train will take off. Some roller coasters use the first hill to pick up speed, which they use for the rest of the ride. Not this one. Kingda Ka starts by accelerating.

In an instant the train shoots forward, pressing riders back into their seats. They are rocketed to 128 miles per hour (206 km/h) in just 3.5 seconds. Some riders scream in delight as the train reaches its top speed. It then starts to climb the hill, 90 degrees straight up.

Kingda Ka speeds toward the first hill.

The train banks to its side as the steel twists toward the top. As it crests the hill, riders are held in place by the restraints. Just as soon as the train reaches the top, it shoots back down. It twists around as it plummets toward the ground. Riders are pressed down into their seats with many times the force of gravity.

Kingda Ka then crests one more hill that is 129 feet (39 m) tall. That's tiny in comparison to the first hill. But just a few decades ago this hill would have

made it the tallest roller coaster in the world. Roller coasters have come a long way in the last 50 years.

In a little over 50 seconds, the ride is over. There are few other places on Earth where riders can go to such extreme heights and speeds in such a short time. For many, the nerves that come with anticipation are worth it!

THE SCIENCE OF THRILLS

Kingda Ka is a major attraction at Six Flags. But it's just one

READY FOR LAUNCH

Kingda Ka's trains are launched with the help of eight hydraulic motors. Nitrogen gas is first compressed inside a chamber. Once the chamber is opened, the gas rushes out and pushes fluid through the motors. These motors then spin and pull a cable hooked onto the train. At peak power, this system makes 20,800 horsepower. A normal car engine makes approximately 175 horsepower.

Kingda Ka hurtles riders up and down a steep, giant hill.

THE WORLD'S FASTEST COASTER

Kingda Ka is fast, but it isn't the fastest coaster in the world. That title belongs to the Formula Rossa ride at Ferrari World in Abu Dhabi, United Arab Emirates. Formula Rossa's train is designed to look like a Ferrari Formula One race car. And it is almost as fast as the real thing. It reaches a top speed of 149 miles per hour (240 km/h) in 4.9 seconds. The coaster's track is also designed like a real-life Formula One track.

of many. Amusement parks such as Six Flags have all kinds of thrill rides. They give people experiences that can't be found anywhere else.

A ride that goes fast is usually thrilling. But thrills are about more than just speed. The way a ride is designed maximizes the fun. Basic laws of science apply to any ride design. Rides that drop riders down quickly provide the feeling of weightlessness. Rides that shoot riders up make them feel like they are astronauts taking off from a launch pad. Amusement park rides can make people feel all sorts of thrilling sensations.

TO NEW
HEIGHTS

Kingda Ka would tower over several world landmarks. The roller coaster stands as tall as a 45-story building. How does this illustration help you understand the thrill of riding Kingda Ka?

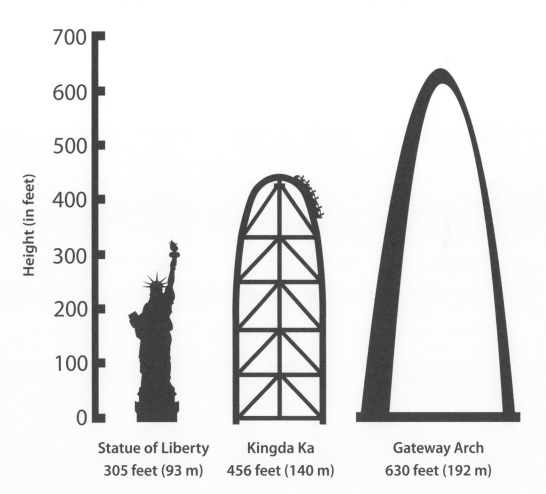

Statue of Liberty
305 feet (93 m)

Kingda Ka
456 feet (140 m)

Gateway Arch
630 feet (192 m)

Designers use science to create thrilling rides.

The forces people experience on rides can be dangerous too. Ride designers have to make sure their ride doesn't subject people to too much force. But it has to have enough force that the ride is thrilling. Finding the right balance of forces is what makes an exciting ride.

STRAIGHT TO THE
SOURCE

This passage from a roller coaster enthusiast describes what it is like to ride the Kingda Ka:

> *After a short wait, the train rolls backwards and latches onto a small "catch car" inside the track. After the train rolls backwards, you know the launch is going to happen within the next 3 seconds, at which point any normal thought process is directed at what the next 28 seconds will be like.*
>
> *Then the train launches. The launch isn't sudden, like you aren't just forced back into the seat suddenly; rather the train thrusts forward and riders are continually pushed back into their seats until the launch is over. It's hard to keep your eyes open during the launch because of the speed that the train is traveling.*

Source: "Ride Review: Kingda Ka." *DoD3*, 2020, thedod3.com.
Accessed 7 July 2020.

CONSIDER YOUR AUDIENCE

Adapt this passage for a different audience, such as your friends. Write a blog post conveying this same information for the new audience. How does your post differ from the original text and why?

SPEEDING DOWN THE TRACK

Not all roller coasters are created equal. Modern coasters such as Kingda Ka get their speed from a launch at the start. But for most of their history, coasters got their speed in a much simpler way. They used a really big hill.

The most basic principle of coaster design is the first hill. A coaster train that isn't launched at the start is slowly pulled up the hill, usually by a chain or cable. The speed a coaster train picks up from rolling down that

A steep hill allows a roller coaster train to pick up speed as gravity pulls it toward the ground.

hill is used for the rest of the ride. So the first hill is always the tallest.

The height of the hill gives a train potential energy. This is the amount of energy an object has available when it is not moving. The taller the hill, the longer the train has to accelerate as it descends and the faster it will go. Also in the equation are the train's weight and the force of gravity pulling the train back to the ground.

When the train crests the hill and starts accelerating to the ground, it starts using that potential energy. The potential energy turns into kinetic energy, which is the energy of motion. At the bottom of a hill, a train has very little potential energy and a lot of kinetic energy. When it goes up a second hill, it trades kinetic energy for potential energy.

One of the laws of physics is that energy cannot be created or destroyed. It can only change form. The form of energy a roller coaster train has changes back and forth many times throughout a single ride.

The energy a roller coaster gets from the beginning of the ride helps it speed through twists and turns.

The transfer of energy is not perfect, though. There are other real-world factors that change the equation. Some energy is always being lost. A train's wheels are always touching the track. This causes friction. Friction is a resistance to movement when two surfaces rub against each other. The coaster track slows the train down because it is not perfectly smooth. High winds can do the same thing.

FEELING THE Gs

Riders feel a lot of thrills while riding a coaster. Some of these thrills are due to gravitational forces, or g-forces. One g-force, or G, is the normal force of the Earth's gravitational pull. More than one G makes a person feel heavier. Less than one makes a person feel lighter.

Coasters use g-forces. Riders feel Gs whenever the train changes direction or speed. Riders feel that force in the opposite direction of travel. They experience the most Gs while speeding through the bottoms of hills. The train is starting its journey upward while gravity tries to pull it back down. Some coasters subject riders to forces of up to five Gs. Ride designers have to be careful. The human body can only withstand so many Gs without getting hurt.

The opposite of that squishing g-force is the stretching g-force riders experience when going over hills. The train throws riders upward as it descends back toward the ground. This force of less than one G lifts them up out of their seats. That is one reason riders need special restraints.

Riders feel g-forces going side to side too. These are called lateral Gs. When the train goes left around a bend, this change in direction throws riders to the right.

Turns on roller coasters are often banked. This means they lean to the side while turning. This replaces the lateral g-force with a g-force down toward the bottom of the car. Rather than throwing riders quickly side to side, the force translates

AIRTIME

Periods of less than one G on roller coasters are sometimes called "airtime." That is because riders come out of their seats and float into the air. Restraints hold them inside the coaster car. A coaster does not have to be the fastest or tallest to give the most airtime. Steel Vengeance at Cedar Point in Sandusky, Ohio, is only 205 feet (62 m) tall and goes 74 miles per hour (119 km/h). But it has the most airtime of any coaster in the world. Riders spend 27.2 seconds of the ride's 2-minute-and-30-second run time in the air.

SWITCHBACK RAILWAY

One of the first roller coasters was a train built to haul coal miners. The mine owners would sell tickets on off hours to tourists. The first coaster built to be an amusement park ride opened on New York's Coney Island in 1884. The Switchback Railway stood 50 feet (15 m) tall and was 600 feet (180 m) long. Its train had a top speed of 6 miles per hour (10 km/h). It was less of a thrill ride and more of a way for riders to get a view of the whole park.

to pushing riders into their seats. Banked turns allow coasters to make turns faster without injuring riders.

LOOPING THE LOOP

People thought of adding loops to coasters soon after the first coasters appeared in the late 1800s. These loops were circular. They were dangerous. The g-forces were too strong. Designers did not understand how to make loops safe. People stopped making coasters with loops.

Looping coasters did not reappear until the 1970s. They were designed with a new loop shape. Rather than

LOOP DESIGNS

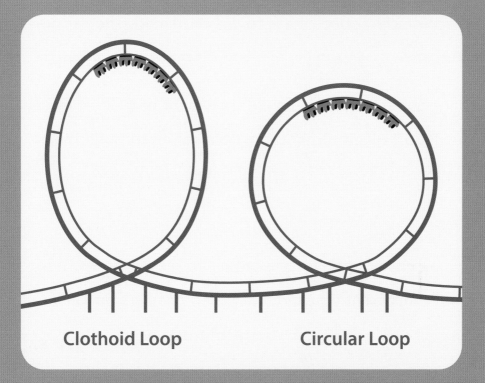

Clothoid Loop   Circular Loop

Modern coasters are designed with clothoid loops, which are shaped like tear drops, instead of circular loops. Take a look at these two designs side by side. How does this help you understand the information in this chapter?

a perfect circle like on early coasters, modern looping coasters have teardrop-shaped loops. This shape is called a *clothoid*.

A circular loop requires a lot more speed to complete the loop. That means riders experience stronger g-forces. The clothoid curve is narrower at the top, which reduces the g-forces produced. The car does not have to go as fast as it would with a circular loop.

Some loops add an extra element of thrill. They can include banked turns so the train spirals through the loops. This type of coaster is called a corkscrew.

READY FOR LAUNCH

Coasters that don't use a big hill to pick up speed must be launched at the start. Launched coasters began to appear in the 1970s. Some of these early systems dropped a heavy weight to pull the train from its starting position. These systems often broke and were not very fast. They could only launch at speeds of up to 60 miles per hour (97 km/h).

Launched coasters became more popular as technology evolved. These coasters became faster in some cases through the use of linear synchronous motors (LSMs). These motors use electromagnetism to power the ride. Magnets have magnetic north and south poles. Opposite poles attract each other. The same poles repel. LSMs use magnetism to first attract a plate connected to the coaster train. As this plate enters the motor, the pole changes to then repel the plate out the other side. A series of motors repeats this process, accelerating the train very quickly.

The first coaster to reach 100 miles per hour (161 km/h) did so in 1997 using LSMs. Not all launched coasters use LSMs. Some, such as Kingda Ka, use hydraulic catapults. Motors quickly pull a chain hooked to the train. However they launch, these rides provide today's riders with greater speeds than ever before.

EXPLORE ONLINE

Chapter Two talks about gravity. The article at the website below goes into more depth on this topic. Does this article answer any of the questions you had about gravity?

WHAT IS GRAVITY?

abdocorelibrary.com/science-amusement-parks

THRILLING RIDES

A roller coaster is just one type of ride at an amusement park. There are many rides that provide different kinds of thrills. They all apply science in their own ways.

Roller coasters have ups and downs, but drop towers take it to the extreme. Drop towers take riders up hundreds of feet in the air on a platform. Once the platform reaches the top, it pauses there for a few seconds. Riders tense up with anticipation.

Drop towers send riders free-falling toward the ground.

DROP OF DOOM

The world's tallest drop tower is attached to the world's tallest roller coaster. Zumanjaro: Drop of Doom is located within the first hill of Kingda Ka at Six Flags Great Adventure and Safari. Zumanjaro's three towers are all 415 feet (126 m) tall. They top out just below the crest of Kingda Ka's hill as trains race by at 128 miles per hour (206 km/h). Riders on Zumanjaro don't drop quite that fast. But they reach speeds of 90 miles per hour (145 km/h) on the way down.

Then suddenly, the platform drops. Riders feel weightless as they free-fall back to the ground, while their restraints keep them in their seats.

The science of a drop tower is pretty simple. Gravity does the work. The experience is a lot like the weightlessness astronauts feel in orbit around Earth.

Italian physicist Galileo noted in the 1600s that all objects fall to Earth at the same rate. It does not matter what they weigh. Even though the platform weighs

Galileo studied astronomy and motion, among other aspects of science.

Some people enjoy the thrill of dropping from great heights at amusement parks.

a lot more than the riders, they fall at the same rate.

Brakes that use the power of magnetism slow the ride

at the bottom. As the platform falls, it passes through

a magnetic field. This field opposes the downward movement of the magnets attached to the platform, slowing it down.

Some drop towers also work in reverse. They shoot riders up from the ground. Much like a space launch, these rides must overcome the force of gravity. In doing so, gravity pulls down on the riders. The combination of gravity and inertia pushes the riders into their seats. Inertia is an object's resistance to a change in motion. One of the laws of physics is that an object in motion will stay in motion. It will keep moving unless another force interrupts it. Likewise a stationary object will stay in place unless a force acts on it. When riders sit at the bottom of the drop tower, their inertia tends to keep them in place, even as the platform begins to rise.

When the ride gets to the top, it free-falls back toward the ground. Riders get a few moments of weightlessness every time the ride drops. These thrill rides offer the best of both worlds.

IN THE SWING OF THINGS

A pendulum is a weighted object that swings from a single point. Pendulums can be found in all sorts of machines. They keep clocks ticking and keep time for musicians. Pendulums can also be found in amusement parks. These rides have names including the Looping Starship or the Screamin' Swing. Pendulum rides all have different kinds of thrills. Some swing riders upside down. Others tumble riders forward and backward. But they all operate on a simple principle.

DROP TOWERS FOR SCIENCE

Drop towers aren't just amusement park rides. They are also scientific tools. Drop towers can simulate the weightless environment of space. The European Space Agency uses a 479-foot (146-m) tall drop tower in Bremen, Germany. The tower provides at least 4.74 seconds of weightless conditions with each drop. Scientists have run more than 5,000 experiments using the tower. It is much cheaper to do experiments there than to send astronauts into space to do them.

Pendulum rides may swing riders upside down.

Pendulum rides use motors to get them started. But once the rider seating area gets high enough, the ride has enough energy built up to keep swinging. As the ride swings, it rubs against the point around which it rotates. It also runs into air particles. These events

Some pendulum rides spin riders in a circle in addition to swinging them.

cause friction. Friction will eventually slow the ride down. It will swing lower and lower until it stops. Motors will need to give it a boost to make it swing higher again.

Some pendulum rides go all the way around in a circle. This swings riders upside down. Once a pendulum swings to its maximum height on one side, gravity pulls it back to the ground. A ride needs a motor to boost it all the way around. These are just a few ways rides use gravity to create a thrilling experience.

FURTHER EVIDENCE

Chapter Three talks about friction. What was one of the main points made about friction? What evidence is included to support this point? The website at the link below provides more information about this force. Find a quote on this website that supports the main point you identified. Does the quote support an existing piece of evidence in this chapter? Or does it offer new evidence?

FRICTION

abdocorelibrary.com/science-amusement-parks

SIMULATING MOTION

Some rides don't even leave the ground. However, they can still give riders big thrills. All the magic happens between the rider's eyes and brain.

A motion simulator ride doesn't go anywhere. But it does move in place. The rider platform only moves a few feet up and down or side to side. It doesn't feel like that, though. Motion simulator rides can

Some motion simulator rides use virtual reality to make it seem like the rider is traveling.

make the rider feel like he or she is flying through space at the speed of light.

These small movements combine with a movie on a screen. This tricks the rider's brain. Riders feel like they are really traveling somewhere.

A GALAXY NOT SO FAR

One of the first motion simulator rides was Star Tours. Star Tours debuted at Disneyland in Anaheim, California, in 1987. The ride has been updated since then. It puts guests on board a ship in the *Star Wars* universe.

Riders sit down and buckle their seat belts. Their spacecraft rises off its base and rockets forward. It dodges enemy spacecraft, flies across

A PRICY THRILL

Star Tours was one of the most expensive amusement park rides ever built. It cost $32 million when it opened in 1987. That was more than it cost to build the entire Disneyland park. Disneyland cost $17 million to build in 1955.

The Millennium Falcon motion simulator ride at Disneyland jostles riders through space as they fly on a mission.

different worlds, and returns safely back home. All that happens without ever really going anywhere.

Rides simulate motion by moving in three directions. They tilt side to side, shift forward and backward, and pivot left and right. They move just enough to fool the brain.

MOTION THEATERS

Another type of motion simulator ride is a motion theater. These theaters sometimes include many sensory experiences to enhance the ride. One example is Soarin' around the World at Disneyland. Guests sit in a row of seats that gets hoisted up in the air in front of a huge video screen. The screen takes up their whole field of vision, making it seem like they are flying over famous world landmarks. They also get wind blown in their faces. Scents of the ground are pumped into the theater to complete the experience.

HOW THE BODY DETECTS MOTION

A motion simulator ride uses three of the body's sensory inputs. The first involves sensory receptors in the body called proprioceptors. These cells send signals to the brain about what position the body is in. They sense the motion of the ride as it tips and turns around. When the body starts to move forward, proprioceptors tell the brain. But these sensors only indicate changes of movement. When the body moves at a constant speed,

The ride Soarin' around the World lets people feel like they are flying over famous world wonders.

the signals stop. Simulators keep moving to keep these signals activating.

The second sensory input involves the vestibular system. The vestibular system, located in the inner ear, is used for balance. It tells the brain if the body is leaning in one direction. The simulator's limited movements help fool this system.

Finally, the brain interprets visual images from the eyes. But the eyes aren't tricked easily. The video must match up with the movements. If it is slightly off, the simulator won't feel real. This can also make people feel sick.

Amusement park rides are evolving all the time. They become bigger and faster as designers look to create new thrills that are still safe for riders. From roller coasters to drop towers, pendulum rides, and motion simulators, science influences each design. With science, even bigger thrills are on the way.

STRAIGHT TO THE
SOURCE

One visitor to Disney World in Orlando, Florida, described riding the simulator Avatar: Flight of Passage. Riders fly on the back of a creature called a banshee from the film *Avatar*. The visitor said:

> *The motorcycle riding position along with gripping the handlebars in front of you make you feel much more like you're a part of the action, especially when combined with the 3D glasses. There was even a moment during the ride where I put my hands up in front of my face because my body was tricked into thinking we were going to run into a charging beast. . . .*
>
> *Restraints come up from behind and rest on your lower back and legs. Air bladders inside the chair inflate and deflate during the ride, giving the impression you're really sitting on a living, breathing banshee.*

Source: "What Makes Avatar: Flight of Passage So Immersive." *Coaster101*, 11 Dec. 2018, coaster101.com. Accessed 3 Aug. 2020.

BACK IT UP

The author of this passage is using evidence to support a point. Write a paragraph describing the point being made. Then write down two or three pieces of evidence used to make the point.

FAST FACTS

- A roller coaster has potential energy at the top of a hill, which becomes kinetic energy as it descends the hill and picks up speed. The coaster train uses this energy to run the course of the ride.

- Not all coasters use a hill to gain all of the speed for a ride. Some are launched coasters that use electromagnetic motors at the start of the ride. These motors attract and then repel plates on a train to rocket the train to high speeds.

- Coasters have loops shaped like tear drops rather than circles so that the trains do not need as much speed to complete the loop, lowering the g-forces the riders experience.

- Drop towers make riders feel the sensation of weightlessness as they drop to Earth.

- Pendulum rides use motors to get going and then the principle of inertia to keep swinging throughout a ride. Some rides also use motors to make a complete revolution in the sky.

- Motion simulator rides stay in place and use a combination of subtle movements and a video screen to create the illusion of motion.

- The body's sensory system sends signals to the brain, and motion simulator rides can trick these senses into feeling movement.

STOP AND
THINK

Dig Deeper

After reading this book, what questions do you still have about amusement park science? With an adult's help, find a few reliable sources that can help you answer your questions. Write a paragraph about what you learned.

Say What?

Studying physics can mean learning a lot of new vocabulary. Find five words in this book you've never heard before. Use a dictionary to find out what they mean. Then write the meanings in your own words and use each word in a new sentence.

Take a Stand

Chapter Four discusses motion simulator rides. As technology evolves, virtual reality may be able to provide the same thrills as riding a roller coaster. Do you think experiencing a roller coaster in virtual reality would be just as fun as the real thing? Why or why not?

Why Do I Care?

Maybe you do not like amusement park rides. But that doesn't mean you can't learn about science by studying them. What are some other real-world examples of the science described in this book? Where else do you see these things in action?

GLOSSARY

accelerate
to change speed

automated
run without
human involvement

bank
to tilt to the side

crest
to move over the top
of something

electromagnetism
magnetism powered
by electricity

hydraulic
powered by a fluid

lateral
side to side

physics
a branch of science
that deals with motion
and energy

sensory
having to do with what the
body sees and feels

simulator
something that creates the
illusion of something else

visual
having to do with sight

ONLINE RESOURCES

To learn more about the science of amusement parks, visit our free resource websites below.

Visit **abdocorelibrary.com** or scan this QR code for free Common Core resources for teachers and students, including vetted activities, multimedia, and booklinks, for deeper subject comprehension.

Visit **abdobooklinks.com** or scan this QR code for free additional online weblinks for further learning. These links are routinely monitored and updated to provide the most current information available.

LEARN MORE

Kenney, Karen Latchana. *Science of Roller Coasters: Understanding Energy*. Abdo Publishing, 2016.

Marquardt, Meg. *Physics in the Real World*. Abdo Publishing, 2016.

INDEX

About the Author

Douglas Hustad is a freelance author primarily of science and history books for young people. He, his wife, and their two dogs live in the northern suburbs of San Diego, California.